A book for all

From Science Learning and Daydreaming

to Self-awareness

By

Javad Kazemi Karbasdehi

Table of Contents

Foreword

This book makes its best to promote enlightenment, create new insights and see the world from another perspective as well as to view the world from above and from a more general perspective, to find ways to achieve self-awareness as well.

Writing causes the thoughts and ideas to remain unforgettable forever and help their dissemination as well. We need to repeat to ourselves every day that *we are a small traveler of time*. Being with our contemporaries, whom we have been lucky enough to meet or benefit from, is a miracle in itself, and our "existence" itself is a miracle, if we really exist in that sense, or even if not have that meaning, and to be like a computer game (in relation to the afterlife) with a set of rules and regulations shaping our future behavior and action, life is still a miracle.

As a free human being and one who is not much captivated with the shackles of this world and has experienced some freedom and emancipation, I can express interesting and new topics that may not have occurred to other human beings at least in some cases, or if happened, they have ignored it. It is better to review the following issues many times in order to both remind and understand more and end up to thinking, developing and spreading new ideas.

An example of a miracle: the fact that if an egg -with which we make a half-boiled or boiled egg- laid by the hen and incubated at a constant temperature for about 21 days, hatches a chick with a beak, legs, feather, nostrils and even a stomach and guts able to digest and excrete food and have blood circulation and respiration, etc. This is a miracle in itself, even challenging Darwin's theory that the order has taken place over millions of years. This theory, despite answering many biological evolutionary questions, is not an inclusive and comprehensive theory, because it takes about 21 days to turn an egg into a chicken, not millions of years. Since such events are assumed *regular* for us, we are not able to understand the miracle and the wonder in it, and we cannot think well about such cases and *ignore* it.

This was just an example; there are many such wonders of nature, such as our own existence or the existence of the universe and many other wonders demanding self reflection. By raising this example in this section and other issues ahead and studying it repeatedly, it is hoped that it will lead to creating a spirit of thinking as well as introducing a philosophy of scrutiny in a simple way.

The following essay has been written in three chapters as follows, which I hope will be beneficial:

1. Elements and natural sciences

2. Biology

3. Daydreaming to self-awareness.

Before addressing the main issue, i.e. daydreaming (fantasy) to self-awareness, it seems quite necessary to raise relevant issues in science. Because it is necessary to philosophize, learn science and knowledge and gain experience in various fields. Learning science and knowledge makes us less delusional in fantasy and actualize self-awareness. Because science defines a framework, it may limit us a little in terms of speed and breadth of thought, and in some cases it may expand the scope.

First Chapter

Elements and Natural Sciences

Galactic science and the science of basic particles and the formation of the elements as well as the elements that make up living things and the concept or meaning of time, light and heat have been my favorite topics that have led to research in these areas, some of which I write the rest of the text to remind myself and to apply it for others to enjoy.

Atoms have strong and weak nuclear energies. Protons in atoms have positive electrical properties, electrons have negative properties, and neutrons have no charge. The strong energy that makes up the nucleus of an atom and brings electrons and protons close together, and the weak energy that holds similar atoms together like iron atoms to form an iron rod. These energies are so intangible and strange that human understanding of the nature of electrons and how they are formed and their nature, as well as the energies between them and the subatomic worlds (quantum), is very limited and limited to the study of how they behave. When an atomic nucleus diminishes, light and heat are generated (like an atomic bomb) or like the sun, which when fused, or a combination of two hydrogen atoms (each hydrogen consists of a nucleus and an electron) together forms a helium atom (helium consisting of a nucleus and two electrons) and the combination of two helium atoms with each other and the formation of other atoms with more electrons such as boron, carbon, oxygen, etc., cause light and heat to be released from the sun and travel a path to us. Reach out and give us energy and life.

So one conclusion or hypothesis could be that it is light and heat that created the sun and other planets and atoms (although a lamp or fluorescent light that emits constant light and heat challenges this hypothesis to some extent that requires research and demands further investigation).

According to astronomers, our sun is ten billion years older, more than four billion years old. In other words, our sun is in its middle age and, like other stars, will eventually explode one day. Its center will become a neutron star or a black hole. The remaining dust or the nebula will lead to the formation of the planets. Stars also reproduce, new stars being born through hydrogen-shaped gas *nebulas*. With the end of hydrogen and helium fuels and the formation of heavier elements, so in a few billion years, the universe will lose its bright stars and become heavier elements that can no longer shine and transmit light and heat, like such a planet as Earth. .

According to many scientists, our world has more than three spatial dimensions and one temporal dimension. Possibly, this theory is correct, and space-time, in addition to comprehensible dimensions, has other small dimensions hidden from view. Imagine a paper that has two dimensions of length and width, but because of its thickness, it is actually three-dimensional that you ignored the third dimension and imagined a smooth two-dimensional surface. The space may also be like this, that is, it has other dimensions that are not visible and understandable due to their small size.

The fact that in atoms the smallest building block of the universe is something called a string again raises the question of what the string itself is made of. Thus, at the smallest scale, there is probably a state of being and non-being, in other words, weak signs of matter or being that are low-energy and unstable and not much different from non-existence. The string will be created on the smallest scale. The boundary between "nothing" and "coming into being from nothing" is defined in the above context so that it may be a way of understanding how this world or God can come into being out of nothing. Now with this in mind, if you are eager to learn about quantum physics, you can go for it.

One of the questions that may come to your mind is how does the world end? Is there a wall at the end of the world and it ends suddenly? If so, what is beyond the wall and beyond the world? One way to escape the answer is to say that the world is infinite. As soon as we say that the world is finite and limited, there is a problem. Maybe, before the end of the world it is like a light shadow that forms around the shadow and becomes less and less clear, that is, it is thinner and different at the end of the world and not in the form of the world we know, and then it reaches its end and then it no longer has meaning, and since it has no meaning, we no longer have to ask what is beyond it.

Formation of carbon and other atoms with more than one electron

Carbon has a nucleus with six electrons, two electrons in the first layer and four electrons in the second layer, the properties of the atoms are repeated in the second layer by eight electrons, and the atoms tend to complete their second layer with eight electrons. This binds and combines atoms with each other to form multiple molecules, of which the carbon atom, due to its four-electron fraction, has the ability to combine with multiple atoms and form the main framework of the most molecular bonds in animals and Food is carbon. In the heart of the sun, due to high heat and pressure, hydrogen atoms combine to form a helium atom with two electrons, helium atoms combine with each other, and so do atoms with more electrons. They make heavier atoms (with one nucleus and more electrons 3, 4, 5, 6, 7, etc.). The heat energy and light released cause the star to become larger and more distant from each other and to dilute it, and when it runs out of nuclear fuel and becomes heavier elements, it suddenly collapses or explodes. As atoms with more electrons are made, in fact, the stars themselves are dying and regenerating. Therefore, we owe our existence to the interactions that exist in the stars, which at high temperatures and pressures cause carbon, oxygen, nitrogen, and other atoms to explode, causing atoms to expand into the universe, and atoms as the basis for the formation of molecules. And all living things are on the earth, so our parents are stars before being assigned to be our father and mother and we do not know the stars in advance. However, the existence of a superior power is also felt in all cases which we call God.

According to scientists, before the big cosmic explosion, physics did not exist in this way and atoms were not formed. Rather, it was after the Big Bang and the expansion of the universe that the atom came into being.

The Light

The study of light was a favorite subject of Albert Einstein and Isaac Newton, who discovered the speed of light in a vacuum and its other properties, but what the nature of the light is and why and exactly how it came into being remains undiscovered. In ancient times, humans worshiped the sun, because it was the embodiment of the light, the heat and existence, the study of the light can expand the imagination and lead us to other sciences and knowledge. The speed of the light in a vacuum is estimated at nearly 300,000 kilometers per second, according to Einstein's Law of Relativity, the laws of physics are relative. For example, the speed of the light in air or water is less than the speed of the light in a vacuum. There is also a well-known rule that energy is equal to the mass of a object multiplied by the power of two velocities ($E = mc \wedge 2$). That is, if a heavy object, such as a spacecraft, wants to reach the speed of the light, it needs infinite energy to achieve the necessary speed and acceleration and reach the speed of the light. What is this light that hits and reflects objects and passes through the pupil of the eye and reaches the retina and is transmitted to the brain through the optic nerve and visualizes a precise and clear image of the objects in three dimensions? Furthermore, if a lot of light is concentrated in one place, like a laser, it will cause a lot of burning and energy emission. It passes through the clear glass. If separated into its constituent lights, it has millions or perhaps billions of different colors with different wavelengths, and it is the different wavelengths that make up the color. Where did it come from? Combining several atoms together and forming new atoms with more electrons in stars produces the light. In fact, it comes from the heart of the atomic particles, according to the above formula that if true, then, the light has mass and may reduce the mass of the stars by spreading light from the stars, but how about fluorescent light and light bulbs through Electric current and the effect on electrons in metal atoms are emitted without reducing its mass? How light is emitted by oscillating the electrons around the atom, while according to modern science, the electron itself is always oscillating around the atom and has no fixed position and does not act like an orbit or the earth's axial rotation around the sun.

Therefore, the exact cause and the nature of the light requires further research. Now, we can hypothesize that if the speed of the light in a vacuum is constant and is close to 300,000 kilometers per second, then until the light is thrown from its origin with a blow or pressure from a certain atom to reach such a speed, it will never be separated from the origin and will not be amplified, and whenever it is amplified, it means that the energy required to reach the said speed to escape the atom has been imposed on it, and therefore, it will reach a constant speed of nearly 300,000 kilometers per second. What this described force is, must be estimated according to Einstein's famous formula, which states that the energy or force is equal to the mass of the object multiplied by the power of two velocities ($E = mc^2$). Whereas, according to the amount the speed of the light, the mass of the light can be used to calculate the energy applied to it, which is another puzzle. On the other hand, if the speed of the light and the energy required to reach that speed are assumed to be constant, then the mass must also be assumed to be constant, while it may be due to the light being facilitated by the fusion of different atoms with more electrons such as Helium, Lithium, Beryllium, Boron, Carbon, Nitrogen and Oxygen, etc. have different masses. The sunlight contains dangerous rays (harmful to humans and animals) such as X-rays, gamma rays, etc., which by the ozone layer (molecules composed of three oxygen atoms) to some extent prevent dangerous rays from entering the earth's surface, each of these lights or rays have different wavelengths and frequencies, Thus, it is unclear whether their velocity or mass may be different because their destructive energy is higher, conceivably only because they are shorter and have more wavelengths (frequencies).

If the light shines from a galaxy or star moving away from our galaxy i.e. escapes from the atom, then the speed of the light that will reach us must be slower and reach us later, and vice versa, if it is not, it means "light" does not escape from the atom, but after being released from the atom by its "cosmic gravitational force", it accelerates to a speed of approximately 300,000 kilometers per second.

The sunlight and light bulbs have one thing in common, imagine a red apple! Whether it is at night and under a lamp or under the sun, it can be seen in red anyway. It should be noted that color is not in apples, but is the reflection of the light through the apple peel, which reflects light in red, because it is the light that has many tints of colors and colors are caused by different frequencies with different wavelengths of light. The spectrum of light in red light has a longer wavelength and the spectrum of purple light has a shorter wavelength. Above the wavelength of red light and below the wavelength of purple light, there are other colors that are not visible to the human eye.

Based on the color of the light emitted from distant galaxies, scientists have discovered that most galaxies are moving away from our galaxy, which is consistent with the Big Bang theory or the beginning of the current universe with a large explosion of hot, very dense matter.

It can be *hypothesized* that it is the light and the heat that make up the stars and other objects as well as the living things (of course, dark energy and the string that connects the entire universe to each other, the force of the gravitation and the force of the atomic gravity and etc maybe follow a different mechanism). Look at your hand, it may be a manifestation of the light and the heat, as well as the stars and everything else between us and the stars. In other words, the primary constituent of the atoms may be the light and the heat, that is, the electrons, protons, and neutrons they are made of it, though in their final layers, because electrons and other elements that make up an atom may first form a specific layer. It, in turn, is made up of finer materials that eventually reach the light and the heat, but the light and the heat may also be made up of other inner layers. The properties of sunlight are in the form of waves and photons (energy packets) that have been and are still being researched extensively by scientists. What is the relationship between the light and the heat with the constituents of the atom as well as the weak and strong atomic forces remain undiscovered.

The Heat

The heat is also a mystery. From a scientific point of view, the intensity of the motion of atoms has been defined as heat. While in the sun, the heat reaches 100,000 degrees, what does the movement of atoms mean at this degree of heat?, and how does this movement melt and burn everything so that it can be transferred? In addition, even the light from a distance contains heat, why does it not cool down and how is it transmitted? It seems to generate heat reaching the destination and hitting the objects, so many questions can be asked that current science needs to address.

Energy is never lost, and the law of thermodynamics in physics has proven it. Energy is transferred from one state to another, such as the heat that is transferred from one molecule to another molecule or atom, for example, a refrigerator that is cold inside. To make cold inside the refrigerator, the environment must be warmer and the heat to air and the earth and the universe is transferred and there is no difference in terms of the heat and the cold in the entire universe. Although it travels in the inner environment of the universe, there is no difference in relation to the whole universe.

The Gravity

The reason why gravitational force works between objects has not yet been proven, and there is only one hypothesis about the function of gravity: " the universe like a mesh or a mosquito net has been intertwined with thin webs and the objects cause traction and subsequently provide a gradient across the space and this curvature causes the gravity and attraction of objects towards one another." Einstein's hypothesis has not yet been demonstrated, but it is the best model for explaining the force of gravity. Therefore, it can be concluded that the whole universe is connected to each other, if it were not connected, there would be no gravitational force, so the gravitational force indicates that objects far apart are actually connected to each other without you being able to see it and you can perceive the force of gravity from the effect it leaves, that is, indirectly, such as the pull of the earth against you and other objects, or the pull amid the earth and the moon, as well as the earth and the sun. This evidence is a good reason to claim that all objects and dark places in the universe are connected to each other. Empty spaces seem empty only to us, because we cannot distinguish the elements or constituents of the empty spaces, but indirectly understand its existence, and so is the existence of a superior and creative power for this wonderful world.

Communications and Radio Waves via Wire and Air

Imagine sitting at home and watching TV, you are probably unaware of how audio and video waves are broadcast on your TV and how audio and video waves are created and stored, then sent through the transmitter and how they are transmitted through the wire or the air, received through the receivers, entered into the TV, and finally analyzed, converted into playable images and sound, and reached your hearing and opinion. In such a way that you have witnessed a clear image with primary colors and clear and high quality sound. All is done at a very high speed indicating the high speed of the waves. These features that exist in nature represent the marvels and wonders of the world that we easily pass by and do not stop to think about because of a process called normalization.

The great scientist Nikola Tesla did research on wireless energies and waves and made advances in this field. According to him, if you want to understand the mystery of the universe, think of concepts such as frequency, energy and vibration.

Two Scientific Scenarios about the Cosmic Destiny in which we Live

One, the Universe continues to expand, and the stars and galaxies will be so far apart that even the light of other galaxies will not reach us, and the Universe will be plunged into darkness, with a temperature minus 273 degrees Celsius on the earth or absolute freezing. The whole world will be frozen and lie at rest. Second, the second scenario is that due to the gravity of the objects in the Universe, the expansion of the Universe decreases over time and gradually begins to shrink, and all the atoms and masses are collected again at one point and turn into a dense, hot gas- like it was before the Big Bang explosion, and it may even explode again and create a new world, and this may happen again and again.

The Time

The time moves like an arrow forward and does not go backwards. Many scientists are conducting research on traveling to the past and/or to the future, but they have not been able to do so far. Space and time are not separate. The time and three dimensions of the space are intertwined so that it can be realized as if it were the fourth dimension (Einstein's General Relativity). According to Einstein's theory contends that if we move at the speed of light, time approaches zero and even in the black holes, in the middle of galaxies, where light cannot escape, time may stop.

We communicate with our future in some way through the writings and the making of tools and the remains of beings, and the future cannot communicate with us in any other way except by examining the remains (including the remains of corpses and fossils) and man-made and ancient writings in the present.

Matter and Antimatter

The computer works with "zero" and "one" instruction, "one" means the power is on and "zero" means the power is off. With these two simple instructions, all the complexity and speed, as well as the variety of computers with high computing capabilities and information transfer and storage of information is provided, the world might have been the same from the scratch and by simple and contrasting instructions it was created and then developed and complicated, which is called "matter and antimatter". Matter and antimatter, despite being very tiny, even thousands of times smaller than the atom, have been created by a superpower that is hidden from view, a vast and wonderful world of particles. A positive unit plus a negative unit if we add together, it becomes zero, that is, nothing. However, each of the positive and negative units has different properties from none and can have different properties from zero or none next to each other and cause variety and complexity, so that they are able to create and shape. Scientists believe that for every substance, there is an antimatter that has exactly the opposite properties of the matter. Although the resultant and fusion of matter and antimatter will again lead to zero and nothing (perhaps at absolute zero temperature or high temperature and pressure), but separately and adjacent to each other has the capability and ability, the creator of this ability should not be forgotten. After death, living organisms decompose again into their constituent atoms, and atoms may, over time and under certain other conditions become finer particles such as the light and the heat, as well as more fundamental constituents to the point that even matter and antimatter, merge together and become nothing. In this world, we are just a small traveler of time wandering in a certain place of space-time (address: Virgo group, local group, Milky Way, Sun, Earth – 21st century) and after a short time disappears. We will go and we cannot predict very distant times well and we do not know exactly what will happen to the planet and the world when we are not. As long as we are alive, it is better to enjoy our lives and know that this short and mortal life is not worth grieving and suffering. I hope all creatures on the Earth and other planets enjoy traveling on a spaceship and moving in the galaxy, and that their journey is fun and entertaining.

With the advancement of science in physics, mathematics, and chemistry, it was science that answered many of the ancient philosophers' questions and the fundamental questions which remained unanswered lead to fatigue and exhaustion. However, in the long run, further development of science left the answer to the fundamental questions of the natural world and theorizing to the basic science, and the modern philosophy turned to sociology, anthropology, human relations, ethics, the observation of science and religion and the contradictions among them produced the expression of literary statements, sometimes politics and states, etc. Thus, to ask about fundamental questions concerning the nature was left it to physicists, chemists, and other scientists so as to provide solutions.

Ideas for Future Research

1- The light emitted from the sun hits the skin and causes the absorption of vitamin D as well as being tanned or sunburned, and by radiating on the plants through the leaves, it causes photosynthesis. It also has millions or maybe billions of different colors (different wavelengths). While the light of a lamp or fluorescent light, seems to follow a different mechanism. Both are lights, but their origin is different. Examining their differences as well as their origin and how they were created will open many doors to human knowledge. Especially since the light emitted from the fluorescent light does not reduce the mass of the metal used in it, while the light emitted from it has its own mass, unless instead of transmitting the mass, it only affects the mass of its surroundings and borrows from it. And the surrounding mass is displaced or just vibrated.

2. Although the sunlight and the light bulbs are very different from each other, but they may be equal in speed of light or have different speeds, the proof of this hypothesis requires further research by the scholars.

3. I see no reason why all electrons should have the same mass, especially at different capacitance layers in atoms, so the latter topic can be investigated.

4. As there are diseases and defects in living organisms and cells, are there defects in atoms and atomic compounds? What is the function of a single electron that is separate from the atom, and is there a single proton or neutron without a nuclear bond, and if so, what is its shape and how stable is it, and where are they found in the world?

Second Chapter

Biology

What is deoxyribonucleic acid, or DNA? The function of DNA: What each cell does and how it behaves is determined by codes that form across a uniform tissue. Each cell reproduces, transmits the DNA code to the new cell, and thus the new cell knows its instructions and functions and cooperates with the other cells. DNA is organized into structures called chromosomes. These chromosomes are duplicated before they divide into cells in a process called DNA replication.

DNA is often compared to a set of maps because it contains the instructions needed to make all the other components of the cell, such as protein molecules and RNA (ribonucleic acid).

DNA, which is the molecule of inheritance and long-term storage of cell genetic information, is composed of carbon, hydrogen, nitrogen, oxygen, and phosphorus atoms in humans and all living things, plants and trees. Also, the amino acid molecule, of which 20 types are known in humans (consisting of the atoms mentioned above), its various compounds have formed thousands of species of protein molecules, and proteins combine with other molecules to form cells. The cells come together to form tissues. Types of cells develop different types of tissues, such as skin tissue, muscle tissue, bone tissue, etc. The body of all living things is made up of cells.

The bodies of all plants, the bodies of all animals, and our human bodies are made up of cells. Humans are also made up of atoms and as a result, the energy described in the first chapter.

Research by scientists has demonstrated that if a human's nuclear energy is released, the power of a large city will be supplied for a week.

Thus, the compounds, Carbon, Hydrogen, Nitrogen, Oxygen, and Phosphorus form the molecules that make up DNA, including the formation of sugar and phosphate as supportings of ladder and four types of amino acids called Adenine, Cytosine, Guanine, and Thymine as steps of ladder. These open types are matched in pairs (adenine molecules with thymine and cytosine molecules with guanine) are intermittently and extensively extended. The length of this strip can be more than a few million molecules. There are billions of ways to arrange molecules in this tape. The multiplicity of arrangements in the DNA molecule causes the multiplicity of diversity of moods, limbs, skin and hair color, height, etc. in humans and other living things.

The DNA molecule attaches to proteins and forms chromosomes. The human body has more than 37,000 billion cells, with 46 chromosomes (23 pairs of chromosomes) in the nucleus of each of these cells. Every human being receives half of his/her chromosomes from his/her mother and the other half from his/her father.

Unlike eggs and the sperm (sex cells), other cells in the body have two sets of identical chromosomes, but eggs and the sperm have one set of each chromosome. During fertilization, 23 chromosomes (not 23 pairs) are transferred from the father's sperm and 23 chromosomes (not 23 pairs) from the mother's egg to the zygote. These 46 chromosomes form 23 pairs of chromosomes, 22 of which determine inherited traits other than male or female sex and are called autosomes. Another pair is called the sex chromosome, which is XY in normal men and XX in normal women.

During the replication process, a copy of DNA is made from its pattern in the cell nucleus, which is one of the basic steps in cell division. During replication, the DNA molecule is passed on unchanged to the next generation. Cells and tissues form and work together in a strange order, which is the same regular formula or programming for life.

Of the more than hundred of natural elements, only 11 elements or atoms contribute significantly to the structure of the living organisms. Most of the atoms in the living system, which are estimated to be about 99%, contain nitrogen, oxygen, carbon, and hydrogen. Sulfur and phosphorus also play important roles, but are not abundant. All of them are in gas mode alone or in combination. Life is made up of the complex molecules that come into contact with these gases. Approximately, 75% of the atoms in the living organisms is made up of hydrogen and oxygen, indicating water in the living systems.

We live in a very mysterious world on the smallest scale and invisible to the naked eye, as well as very large and seemingly infinite. A huge world in which not only is the man very tiny, but the Earth, the Sun, and the Milky Way Galaxy are nothing more than small particles. Human knowledge of atomic constituents and energies, the mechanism of gravity, the size of the Universe, and the operation and the nature of the black holes at the center of the galaxy is scant. As a famous example, the baby stays in the mother's womb.

An animal or plant cell is known as the smallest unit of life. All the living organisms on the Earth have four basic attributes in common, including cellular organization, growth and metabolism, reproduction and inheritance. Cells, like DNA and other molecules, are made of atoms, so tissues, organs and our whole body and all the animals and the plants and even the proteins, lipids (like fat) and carbohydrates (like sugar) are all made up of atoms. Different properties and DNA or cell code lead to the formation of different cells such as cells of different components of the eye or different cells of blood or cells of blood vessels, bones, hair, skin, liver, kidneys, spleen, intestines, vocal cords, lungs, etc. They have become human bodies, which is like a miracle. The result is the juxtaposition of cells, tissues, and organs into a complete human body whose entire components are in close harmony with each other in such a way that they provide survival, such as digestion of food and conversion into energy and excretion. Disposal of waste, breathing and delivering oxygen to all the cells to survive and react to risk factors as well as the function of hormones and enzymes at the right time and in the right place, etc. If there were not such numerous coordinations, various parts of the body would not be able to survive for a moment. That is, from very small atoms with little variety, intelligent beings have emerged who are able to see the nature and the world around them, as well as to know and also to reach self-awareness of the world that creates them. These wonders excite and make men think. The intelligence in the subconscious of cells, genes, and DNA of the living things seems to be stronger than the conscious intelligence of our brain. Most intracorporeal reactions are almost involuntary, such as the reaction of the white blood cells to microbes and the production of antibody to prepare for similar microbes in the future, or the spontaneous healing of wounds or blood clots, and many others. Involuntary actions that indicate unconscious intelligence. Most importantly, the creation of a complex human being with diverse cells and different organs and even in harmony with each other only originates from a single cell, which shows intelligence and tact.

The most complex machine in nature is the body of the living things, especially humans. If there is no coordination with the whole body anywhere in the body, the machine will have serious problems and in most cases may be completely disrupted. This harmony and order have emerged among all the components within nine months. At the same time, with the growth and development of new cells and organs, there is a special harmony and order between the formation and the establishment in suitable neighborhoods and also not disturbing the order and life of other components. For example, without the development of some components such as the heart and arteries, the liver, kidneys, brain, endocrine glands and bones may not form yet, but start at the right time and settle in the right place, as well as order and life inside. The cells themselves are thought-provoking at the time of their first creation. Timing, priority, and tardiness are especially important in the formation of components, as well as in growth, and development, as well as in overall harmony and order, in order to proceed according to plan and not to ruin the whole work. Then, all these cases are related to each other and interact and become autonomous. It seems necessary that all these items are pre-arranged and precise. After the completion of the work and the final completion, a complex and autonomous device has been created that is able to swallow, digest, breathe and convert into energy and other things that have made possible the continuation of life, which requires a harmony and order and interaction. It is all the components that are pre-embedded, although after order it will move towards disorder which is also normal and the whole world looks like this, everything will move towards disorder after the order to adapt to its surroundings so that the whole world or the surrounding environment becomes homogeneous. We will become like the soil of the earth again and turn into our constituent atoms. This homogenization can be seen in other places as well, such as the movement of cold and dense air towards warm air, or the movement of river water downhill, or the movement of concentrated material towards diluted matter in the blood and in the interstitial space among cells and so on. The re-transformation of man into its primary constituents is natural because, firstly, it is composed of atoms, and secondly, with a special order that is outside the order of the surrounding nature, and with a harmony it has become something whose concentration is higher than the surrounding environment. It is and will inevitably lead to disorder, and this is also due to the law of motion because the whole universe is in motion.

Iron ions in hemoglobin red blood cells, like a peak, absorb oxygen from the lungs and carry it through the blood to various parts of the body and to the cells, indicating the use of this chemical reaction in order. Other uses of iron ions in the body include the production of hemoglobin in the blood and resistance to stress and illness and the proper functioning of enzymes, as well as strengthening the immune system.

In addition to the planning and order mentioned at the time of the creation of the living things, the post-creation coordination within the body as well as in relation to the environment such as respiration and nutrition and the disposal of waste is amazing. In terms of respiration, gases in the air mainly contain nitrogen, as well as oxygen and carbon dioxide gases and other gases in the air, among which oxygen has the ability to react chemically with sugars, fats and proteins, such as carbon, oxygen. Hydrogen is broken down to produce water, carbon dioxide, and the energy needed by cells. Carbon dioxide reaches the lungs through the blood in a certain order and is excreted through exhaled air. Carbohydrates (such as sugars, including glucose) and fats and proteins in the blood have already reached the body's cells through nutrition, digestion, and circulation. All of these are chemical reactions that lead to the storage and release of energy by combining atoms in nature and then breaking them down in the living organisms. The human body is able to use energy and convert it into kinetic energy, thinking, heat and other things, in other words, it uses and adapts atomic energy for its vital benefits and needs.

After making all these harmonies, living organisms have reached a self-awareness of their environment and the entire universe and the science in it, as well as their constituent factors. The science and laws of nature already exist and the man only discovers and applies them.

Sugar, including glucose, is produced in plants through water, carbon dioxide, and sunlight. In plant leaves, due to sunlight in the green profile of plants, it leads to photosynthesis, during which sugar is formed by combining three atoms of carbon, oxygen and hydrogen.

Note that the air you breathe, like some of the oxygen and nitrogen in it, is caused by the decomposition of the bodies of former living things, and such cycles in nature cause diversity as well as the possibility of survival. In other words, some movements in nature are rotational.

According to Richard Dawkins' book "The Selfish Gene", genes create machines that are the body of the living things to evolve, even though each individual is unique and dormant, but by reproducing and continuing its life, a gene is actually immortal or at least long-lived. From this point of view, genes and DNA are strange and scary creatures, and we are just a machine for the formation and extension of DNA life. The genes do their best to survive in order to protect the car they are driving through the structure of satisfaction and pleasure, as well as the bad feeling and pain of danger and destruction, and even to continue surviving when the machine is worn out. The body reproduces sexually and asexually, so it has a longer lifespan than the body machine. Genes, which are the formula for directing and controlling all cellular and mechanical activities of the body in animals and plants, also steer and control their behavior and influence their performance. What we already put forward probably indicates the reason and origin of selfawareness.

Chapter III

Daydreaming to Self-awareness

Imagination is the fastest thing in the world and it also requires theorizing. Self-awareness means that nature is able to know and understand it, and even beyond that, it can be aware of its Creator.

Adherence to our world and body (forming habits and then neglecting)

The meaning of the worldy attachment (sticking to it and then being oblivious) is much broader than it can be explained in a few sentences or pages, but here I will write a brief account of what comes to my mind:

This world leads to dependence because of its lure, its appeal and tantalizing expression, and due to the smoke that blocks our eyes and prevents us from seeing the truth, so inevitably all of us in this world are relatively unaware and confused. We are not willing to stop clinging to the world. We move along the river and we are not used to swimming in the opposite direction. Sometimes, we become so preoccupied with ourselves that we fall into a void of thought and delusion and pursue only personal goals and interests, and to achieve that, we set foot on many things or close the doors on many things. We are unaware of what it would think of us if the world and the universe had eyes and saw us. One of the reasons we become dependent on the world is because we are made up of the same materials that made up the world, and at the same time we are unaware of this. Since we take care of our physical and spiritual needs to continue living, and dependence and attachment to the world seems essential for our survival, so it causes us to drown or neglect in this world. We are so immersed in the world and of ourselves, we think the world is just this street or this city or this country and this planet. We think of the earth as our eternal world, we are oblivious to many things, we are trapped in the atmosphere, we have little aspect and capacity, all of these are signs of being deceived in this world. In the hope of the day when we wake up from the slumber of negligence and become more and more unconscious towards self-awareness. We are all unaware in this world; Depending on the nature and splendor of this world and the satisfaction of personal or collective needs that have tendencies that lead man towards him and are institutionalized in us, and that is how to be free (regardless of social norms and laws, etc which restrict freedom), we turn away, we flee from death, and we are afraid of it because we do not experience death. By their death, each living thing actually gives others a chance to enter this world and experience this world.

Of course, getting used to this world and negligence, does not necessarily take us away from being free, but in some cases it gives a sense of freedom, for example, for a rural boy due to the mental vacuum in childhood but still in freedom. Being truly immersed, it seems that living in the countryside and in the heart of the nature and wandering freely and doing *unwise* and *irrational* things and also living in the present time is a reason to be free and taste the joy of heaven, but for one who has experienced that time and tasted the joy of heaven in childhood will no longer see a unique paradise, and in middle age, by distancing oneself from negligence and mischief, life will be more difficult because the feeling of being driven away reaches the man from heaven.

Whether a person enjoys swimming in a small, dirty river as a child, or feels good about killing small animals, and feels free is due to unconsciousness and emptiness in thought, if he ever knew how dirty the river water is. It would not swim and thus, was deprived of some pleasure. So, covenants and the growth of thinking and self-awareness usually cause us to limit ourselves and not do certain things and as a result do not enjoy some of the pleasures of life. The less we think about the consequences of work and the more we live in the present, the more we even face social anomalies, the less complexes and mental deficiencies are emptied. This may sound bad, but it is true. Apparently, we must always be in a series of ignorance and shortsightedness in order to achieve pleasure in this world, in other words, to be deceived by this world and to lose ourselves a little in order to find things. In some cases, to go with the stream and also been obsessed with this world will cause more joy, pleasure and peace, if do not adjust yourself with the ups and downs of the life, the life will also start to disagree with you.

Man-made facilities and advances in technology increase the well-being of society, but the evidence around us does not support this theory. We have emerged from the heart of nature and are a part of it and nourish it and return to it in the end.

It is worth noting Kafka's famous novel "The Metamorphosis", in which the character of the novel transforms from a human into a large insect and descends to a lower level than before. He is not surprised to find that he has become a giant insect, and after a while, he accepts it. In fact, he tries to adapt his life to becoming a big insect, and he knows that he must gradually accept his family's hatred for him. He knows that with this *metamorphosis* he will become the only hated creature in the house, but he wants to cope with this situation. Knowing that he has become a full-fledged insect, he tries again to get on the train to get to work. If he does not seem to understand his situation and what is important only at that moment is to get to work. What he does every day.

We, humans and even other animals, move away from the real self as we might be, by dissolving into society, civilization, and culture, and being attracted to the environment around us. We all turn away from the real self, we might be and lean in one direction. This change of direction and movement in different directions can be the reason why we are like a raw tablet in which the world around us begins to cocoon and draw patterns and gradually determine our overall perception and behavior. Sometimes, with a moment of reflection and the use of ingenuity and self-awareness, we may discard a large amount of our old prejudices and thoughts and replace them with new things, however, it still seems we are entangle in a fish jug. We must also be careful to know the illusion and not deceive ourselves because it causes us to get caught up in an illusion and assume that the illusion is real, that it is worse than a vacuum in thought.

Tendency to Beauty

Living beings are amazed and surprised to see or feel the order, color, and the combination of colors, patterns, and cohesive shapes, as well as the intelligence and subconscious that have been present in the genes since birth. And there are our regular cells, it creates excitement and joy, and this intuitive perception causes the creation of a sense of aesthetics in the conscious as well as the subconscious, and no matter how much this sense of aesthetics is strengthened, eventually you become a creature with beautiful thoughts. In this case, we can hope that within you, the beauties will finally overcome the ugliness, and as a result, the good will dominate the evils, and this is how we feel that each of us is inside. We have an inner messenger or a prophet who gives us the power to distinguish good from evil. Scholars and scientists are usually expected to be able to better distinguish good from evil. Other factors such as humanity and love for children and feel affection for other creatures and other factors can also be effective in distinguishing good from evil, e.g. the other is that we feel good as the source of our peace and comfort and evil or bad as the source of our fears, pains and problems that are formed in the social and cultural dimension. Now, we can better understand why the god of evil has weakened in the evolution of the religions and has turned into the devil and has become a creature of the god of good, because we prefer to be relieved with the idea that the good will eventually overcome the evil.

When certain ideas and thoughts penetrate your subconscious and set in and institutionalize over time, and the interactions between the subconscious and the conscious occur, you must have the power to distinguish the good from the evil. There is a suspicion that the food of the mind or the soul in the universe is more than it is involved in. In any case, when we are a small child, the brain wiring is not yet inclusive, moreover, our brain is not a good commander due to the lack of experience and knowledge of the world, and the memories of that time are hard to remember or do not remember at all. Thoughts and feelings are imperfect, and it is education and life experience that enters the subconscious and long-term memory and control and guide us.

In his book "Brain Evolution", Joe Dispenza believes that the subconscious mind preceded the brain and matter and already exists. There are also philosophers who believe in the cosmic intelligence .

Of course, according to Darwin, this cosmic intelligence or spirit can be challenged, or without challenging and looking at it from the perspective of how it combines atoms and forms larger and more complex molecules, And then there is the natural selection, which causes dysfunctional, weak, incompatible forms and images to be removed, leaving only the regular and compatible with the environment, however, Darwin's theory has no explanation for the mind and the soul.

Man and the Sublime Man

A fundamental problem with becoming a human is that human beings also have animal qualities and instincts, and at the same time each person prefers his own personal interests to the interests of others, so becoming human is not only associated with interests and pleasure, it can also present shortcomings and weaknesses, especially morally and collectively, so in order to evolve into a different human being and to evolve into a sublime human, and also to move away from egoism and selfishness, we have to distance ourselves from being an ordinary human and get rid of our animal nature and become a creature that has some animal or human characteristics, but become a creature that is far from expectation from the point of view of an ordinary human being due to intelligence, self-sacrifice and the power of love and affection. This means liberation and freedom, so that we may become more attractive and beloved to others, and in some qualities, such as love and self-sacrifice, more progress may be made. Being human creates problems and conflicts with idealistic goals and being human. To become human intellectually and morally and to be thoughtful requires hard training and also requires deterrents such as religion or law, in addition to values and prejudices as well as the goals and the beliefs, etc. All this must be learned very quickly in a short period of life in this world with experience and education and being in civilization and culture. Exaltation may at any time or often take you away from worldly pleasure and recreation, and may require special circumstances, such as the belief that the world is the abode of the hereafter, and in this world we are to suffer hardships to achieve happiness in the next abode. I hope this process of suffering hardships will not continue in the next afterlife dwellings.

In the light of the governments and the markets and the evolving constitution which has replaced the old empires, communities and civilizations are living in a relative convenience and security, and the order is being sustained. The existence of the state is as essential as the father of a family. Now, a noble human being can find himself in the civilization and culture in which he grew up or lives and determine his own path. The sublime man finds meaning in the interaction and existence of other living beings. Outside of our inner conscience and at the community level, the meaning of morality and perhaps feelings and emotions find meaning, but at the same time it erupts from our inner conscience and this is a two-way communication. It has probably happened to you that when you laugh face to face in the presence of your friends, then your friends also laugh or smile involuntarily. Your feelings are induced to the other side, so happiness and misery as well as despair are all interdependent. I like the saying that "what you do not like for yourself, do not like for others, and what you like for yourself, like for others" that if this rule is observed in most people in a community and smaller groups, then the collective decisions, like the individual decisions of some noble human beings, will lead to the good of all the members of that group and possibly the whole society. Some people do not believe in making individual decisions for the group.

Love and feel affection for the human beings and animals and even nature, because the whole universe is interconnected and the result of your actions towards others and the world around you will return to you in different forms.

Self-awareness in Cells

Cells and molecules are located in dark places in the body, but at the same time they perform their assigned tasks efficiently while they have no eyes, ears or nose and are located in a dark place.

The cells of the body that are located in the tissues are immersed in the interstitial water, even inside the cells, there is water that provides the food and chemical exchanges of the cell with its surroundings and inside the cell itself. Due to the presence of this interwoven water, which allows the exchange of food, oxygen and other chemicals in the blood vessels and cells. In fact, food and oxygen travel through the blood to the interstitial water and waste products to the interstitial water. Blood vessels move and are displaced and eventually excreted. Thus, from the point of view of the animal cells, the gods constantly provide them with food and oxygen and also excrete wastes, but the cells do not know who these gods are, for whom they have provided the blessing. In fact, cells that are located in a specific place and immersed in interstitial water prepare all their biological needs around them and are replenished after reduction, without realizing how the gods provided them with such a gift. Even we do not know for sure and we feed only to satisfy the need of hunger and thirst or for pleasure and fun and usually we do not even think that by doing this we nourish the cells of our body.

Without being aware of the story and the whole story, the cells can eventually come to the conclusion that there are gods who provide them with food on a regular basis. They may even be unaware that the food has reached them through the bloodstream, but if one day they communicate with other cells, they may get alert and may attain some facts. Understand, for example, that the bloodstream that carries food to them is a tool of their own, consisting of component atoms with different mechanisms and functions, and that they receive the materials they need after a process. Such self-awareness of cells may seem unlikely, but not impossible, at least in the case of viruses and bacteria that have been able to multiply and continue to reproduce and even evolve. Destroying previously pathogenic microbes is a sign of memory and self-awareness on a smaller scale than a complex animal. It is very difficult for a cell made specifically for the eye to understand what it was created for and who it serves, and what the next consequence of this service is, and so are each of the other cells, but in general and they work together as a collection with strange harmony and accord, so they are very smart. They even have births and origins, but eventually, over time and after the initial stages of development, they then enter the phase of aging and disorder. It exists not only in cells or the living things, but also in objects and matter, because motion, energy, and vigor are also present in atoms. Thus, as science advances in the fundamental particles that make up the bodies and beings, we become closer to the existential depths of self-awareness and unconsciousness.

By comparing the artificial intelligence that does not have a coherent understanding of space and time as well as color, shape and smell, and humans can make progress in finding the source of self-awareness in the living things. Like cells in the dark, consciousness emerges from dark places and emerges, and from materials that are physical and chemical, perceptual and sensory experience are created.

Among the current concerns of scientists (scholars), I think the most important ones are two: one, the discovery of the living organisms on the planets other than the Earth, and two, the discovery of where does self-awareness come from in the living organisms?, and what is the meaning of life ?, and what is the rationale and emotion? Artificial intelligence is encoded with zero and one, but how is the human brain encoded? Regarding thinking and emotions, biologists have discovered that the chemical activity is caused by a potential difference among the atoms of sodium and potassium, which have positive and negative charges and move by their motion. Electromagnetic cells in the brain cells, and these electromagnets create the ability to think and feel.

René Descartes, the well-known mathematician and philosopher, said that "I think then I am", in a simple way and through intuitive certainty, wanted to say that there is something, and there is at least one external reality and even considered it as a proof of the existence of God.

Humans are judged by the circumstances in which they are situated

Every human being is born to a certain family and has special talents and abilities and lives in a certain geographical environment and climate. Many factors such as his precedent or bittersweet memories creates a special view of this world and of others. So, the test of human beings is done in different situations and we should not judge others for theft or other anomalies, maybe if we walk in that person's shoes the same behavior and deed are produced by us, and possibly even more intensely, so it is better not to judge others, as the saying goes, "If they are ordered to arrest the drunk, they should get whoever is in the town." Should a person who steals to feed his hungry children be treated the same as someone who is well-off but commits robbery to amplify his/her wealth? Undoubtedly, God will use a special scale to conclude on the Day of Judgment and Accountability in order to administer justice to human beings, according to their specific circumstances. To prove the correctness and goodness of the existence of Adam and Eve and the creation of man. It is better to be a good mirror for our reflection in this world and not to forget that even if we are not, the world still exists. The question also arises as to why we should be in order for a being to know and testify that the world exists. Our memories are very influential in our lifestyle and behavior, for example, if we are ostracized by someone or oppressed by people, or we live in a society where everyone thinks only of themselves, then we may choose to go with the stream. Other elements affecting our behavior are our foresight and our goals. We may go to great lengths to achieve our goals and put our own interests ahead of the interests of others. Justice does not necessarily mean equality. The idea that justice shall be practiced equally does not necessarily apply in all cases, because sometimes justice requires some people to benefit more, because according to the merit and effort of each person, his share must be different in order for the true justice to be properly practiced, nevertheless, caution should be taken as much as possible, and the share of people should be as close as possible and with less differences, so that the rights of the oppressed may not be lost. Therefore, establishing justice is a very difficult task, because it is a matter of judgment and also relative, and it may be different from the point of view of different people, and it depends on the spiritual and psychological aspects of human beings and human civilization and culture.

Time and Space Limits

One of the reasons we forget that we are a small time traveler is that we think we will not die and we will live forever. We do not believe that one day we will pass away and our bodies will be succumbed to dust. As the saying goes, "Eventually, we will turn into the pottery clay of the potter". Since, we were primarily a child and then we developed and grew older and became middle-aged and elderly, this process takes a long time for us because it has brought about many transformations while 70 years of life versus unlimited time or moment. Longer is a diminutive. Of course, the human race has been and will continue to exist, and in this sense, the human life is longer, especially since our knowledge of the far-away past, to some extent of the future, as well as remote distances in galaxies, knowing history, pushing our science beyond the time and the place and possess more knowledge than our age and modify the time and the place to some extent.

As we became more limited in space and only experienced as much as we age, and limited to, our place of residence or our city or country, our useful life could be longer than our age during our lifetime. With the help of various media such as television, computer, radio, books, articles, newspapers, etc. We obtain images and information from different parts of the earth and the world, such as space photographs and the results of scientists' research. Knowledge is passed from generation to generation, and through learning science, writing books, articles, as well as educate children, future generations travel on the track of science and knowledge of the past generations and benefit from their experience and inventions, and their civilization and the society turn out to be more advanced. And they are more civilized, they may even boost intelligence, letters, vocabulary and sentences, the sophisticated and sympathetic society of today owes this gift to its ancestors who lived like other animals until 10,000 years ago. In addition, through the blessings of thought and imagination, one can go to far places and times or achieve many meaningful topics which are even beyond the present time and place.

The present is the future relative to the past, and the future is the result of our own actions and desires in the present, which shape our future. Our thoughts are related to the past and the future, otherwise, we would not regret the past and be attached to the future, it is the attachment to the future that makes us want to survive, and it is the experience of the past that influences the policy of the future. Past experience and future policies determine how we reflect and behave in the present. Thus, we mentally travel in the past and in the future, of course, this journey or thinking takes place in the present, we are not physically able to move the body from the present to the past and the future, and the time is moving forward like an arrow.

Perception of the beauties and the grasp of meaningfulness cause free and abandoned human beings, not to feel drained and not to stop moving. You can enjoy living.

Right now is the future in relation to the past

Making money and making good use of money is fine and sensible, but we are not born to just make and save money, we make money to live more comfortably and enjoy more facilities and relax, then, we have to utilize money. We accumulate wealth to enjoy in the future, but unaware of the fact that the present, in other words, this instant, is the future of the past, and deprive ourselves of the pleasure while the future on the horizon may never come, so we learn to live like children in the present. Let us fret less and stop regretting the past and worry less about the future live in the moment and rejoice and get pleasure from the world before it is too late or when there is no more opportunity or desire. Some things are enjoyable at the same time, such as watching an animation like when were a child, or going on a trip and driving at a young and middle age that you will not feel when it passes. There is more adventure and curiosity in traveling at a younger age.

In addition to the fact that we are a small traveler of time, we are also on the path of evolution due to the historical and biological course, and this evolution is going on biologically, culturally, ideologically as well as scientifically. The creatures have to go through the time as well as the reproduction to get in touch with their full version. In this way, we can hope that this coming and going is not for nothing but to become a perfect version of ourselves.

Are there other worlds below the atomic or beyond the Universe or in our vicinity?

The answer to the above question is very difficult, but it is theoretically thought-provoking. Given the wonders and intricacies of the atom and the subatomic world, it is no exaggeration to say that there may be worlds different from the world we are familiar with and figure out what is beyond our comprehension, because we are limited. And we live in our own tangible and perceptible world that is perceived by the five senses while the atom itself is made up of other particles and energies that we know very little about, the nature of the energy and the particles that make it up, and we know very much about the quantum world. It is minute, so we still do not know what rules and regulations prevail in that (subatomic) world. What creatures with what characteristics can be created in that world? What is the relationship between the light and the heat and the pull inside the atom with the quantum world? We are so inadequate and ignorant, we cannot even prevent our own death, and our birth was not our own choice either. We know nothing of the afterlife. Why we are here at this time, being contemporary with our contemporaries is a miracle in itself, and why there is a reason why we must live in such a time and place according to geographical and temporal determinism. With our death and the destruction of the whole earth and its creatures, what happens to the world in which we live, what difference does it make to the world if we are not, we who cannot intervene in this world except our own planet and ultimately our own galaxy. We are much smaller than that.

When it is possible to create life through the living cells, i.e. atoms, then superior power can create world from other elements or atoms other than the atoms currently used, through various compounds or rules, and Also, the use of the other atoms, such as iron, gold, copper, etc., in addition to each of the possible beings, can be created in the same world and in other galaxies or other worlds with different properties from our visible world, the worlds which our eyes, ears and other five senses are not capable of perceiving and observing. There will be different meanings, perceptions and awareness, for example, maybe something called pain no longer has meaning, so the feeling of empathy, help or even a common feeling towards the same species and animals, or even love and affection will fade away and instead the rules and other principles should rule, such as: immortality, absolute obedience to a superior power and being responsible for doing a certain job, or drowning in a constant joy and all the unknown or incomprehensible things that are not realized and described. Other worlds may even be near us but not recognizable by the five senses or man-made devices, and if so, in the form of waves, light, or electricity, or anything like dark energy, otherwise, we have expected, while the truth is different from the reality we imagined. Maybe, we were not made to understand them, but only to live in our own comprehensible reality, to enjoy some things and live the same routine for a few mornings, then die and leave the game of life to our heirs and grandchildren to follow this process and the divine routine or ordeal is experienced over and over again at different times, by various civilizations, and under dissimilar circumstances, and ultimately leads to a conclusion. These divine experiments can be performed on the creatures created in other worlds at the same time, or perhaps after the destruction of this world, another world is created and the tests continue again to finally determine the best world and the best creatures.

It is not necessary for only the best creatures to be immortal, because the universe can be so large or so many different worlds that all creatures live in it, without even knowing each other. But immortality requires conditions and characteristics different from our present world, such as, no aging happens in it, and there is no possibility of injury or loss of limbs, or even the need to eat and breathe. All of which require the absence of the limbs. If there are organs (limbs) and the possibility of defects, then immortality requires rapid regeneration and renovation or reproduction. With each reproduction, old memories are erased and a new character is reshaped, but immortality is still in jeopardy because of the dangers of destroying the world or the planet, unless the supreme power has devised a solution to all of this.

The good or the greatness of one type of creature is not a reason for the destruction or non-creation of other creatures, so it is better for other creatures to be created and be tested or re-engineered and modified creatures to reveal more facts about the superior power. Of course, the poor test subjects may curse me for such an offer, because in order for something to become clear to themselves and their Creator, they have to be trialed and tested many times, and in the end it is not clear what awaits them. I myself am afraid of the suggestions I give for the superior power, maybe it is better that we do not interfere in the work of God and become our servants. But since man was created free, let us at least think freely and get rid of the limitations and fences we have built around us, in other words, become aware. Move from the unconscious to the self. While enjoying the splendor of the world, would not be deceived by appearances.

Life in this world is like a computer game against the beyond

In this world, it is as if the smoke has blocked our eyes from understanding the truth. Whether or not we really exist, is a very difficult and challenging question. What is the difference between reality and truth? When we look at different colors of light, different colors are actually different wavelengths of the light, which is true, but the fact is that we think of it in different colors. We compare the heat with our body and imagine, for example, 10 degrees Celsius as cold and 45 degrees as very hot. From a scientific point of view, it is the movement of molecules or atoms of objects. From the point of view of the sun, for example, it is 1000 degrees cold, but 100,000 degrees hot. Everything we imagine or perceive, then, is not necessarily the truth of the matter, but merely an inner reality or pattern for our perception of our surroundings through the five senses. In a device that has three directions (length, width, and height), if you place the zero point in place, you can determine the position of a point or an object in space, but if you move the zero point, the position of length, width, and the geographical altitude of that point or object will also change. The reality of objects from our point of view may be different from the reality from another point of view, and the truth is something else.

We live in a world that we have perceived in our own way with our five senses and is personalized with our own realities, with scientific advances our perception of some things changes and perhaps gets closer to the truth. Science is only the best model and formulation of reality and it stands until a better model or explanation is found.

We have many emotions such as anger, love, affection, hatred, jealousy, revenge, resentment, hunger and so on. All our emotions are in fact a set of rules or rules of life that cause us to make different reactions and decisions in different situations. By knowing more about human personality, one can predict their reactions and behavior.

Somewhat like the laws of physics that God created and then it seems as if He is asleep and do not thinking about the future of the Creation, because He knows what He has created and in which direction they are destined to move and what will happen in the end. Therefore, there is no need to interfere in the affairs of nature and the world, and the nature is moving in a predestined array in a predetermined direction, and from God's point of view, it can be predicted. We are like a game and a toy so that our words, thoughts and behavior determine the possible consequences of laws such as our emotions. The game starts from the moment of birth and continues until the moment of death, and its product, which has a large number of human samples and the average of all of them shows the result of the essence of creation and the true nature of the creature called man, these rules apply to other animals. It is very interesting to know that the planet also plays an important role in this game of life, because if the rules were set in a different environment and nature, then the possible consequences of the rules would change and even the rules might change. Thus, different events and happenings took place and human beings were tested under simpler or more complex conditions and situations. Since each of us was born into the world with empty and zero memories and no one has communicated with the people of this world after death, it is not unlikely that they will be further tested in another world.

One of the most important laws in this world that all human beings are involved with is that " pain sufferer is a doctor". This may not be the case in other worlds, and other laws may prevail instead which do not require suffering. Other laws that may exist in other worlds include the power to know everything about others or abilities that test the capacity and aspect of human beings. Knowing the generalities and seeing things from above gives us more control and a more complete view of our thoughts and behavior. There are other exercises besides hurting or helping others or remembering God in life which help guide people; like loving and having children, which makes a person forget to live only for himself, and through family ties, he achieves social ties and becomes more civilized, and moves away from egoism and selfishness.

Why, when we dream, do we think that it is the same as reality and that it happened in the real world? Sleep is visible in our subconscious mind, in a higher layer of the subconscious when we wake up we are still in the higher layers of the subconscious but we still think that this is the truth and that everything is the same truth and we are unaware, we fall asleep again and live in the subconscious mind. It is rare to realize in the dream world that this is just a dream, but every time in the dream world, I hesitate that I am dreaming, and this is just a dream. When you dream, many impossible and wonderful things happen that seem extraordinary or strange, such as running very fast or even slowly, as well as lifting heavy objects and walking long distances on the ground in a short time and many other things that seem unusual to us and become possible in a dream are like a miracle, but now in the waking world many things in this world will be like a miracle and unusual to us, such as water, soil, air and the creation of living beings through atoms and elements, as well as the rotation of the earth around the sun and the sun around the galaxy and the movement of galaxies in the universe. So that we exist and we die and we go back to our original constituent atoms and we have the nightmare of death, if we wake up (after death) then we say what a relief it was just a dream and it was not true. But at any time, while dreaming, you may realize that you are dreaming, you may also realize in this world that this is just a dream. From the strangeness of the events in the dream, it can be understood to some extent that it is a dream, and the wonders of this world, which are very mysterious and enigmatic, guide us towards the dream of this world. That is, the wonders of this world are itself a guide to its dreaminess, like the rotation of the earth around the sun or like the existence of the universe and our existence in this world, all of which are a mystery.

The Last Prophet

Prophet Mohammad (PBUH), who is the last prophet according to Muslims, at the age of forty, preached the worship of God and the divine religion, and recited the Qur'an after the age of forty. The fame and reputation of the Prophet Muhammad (PBUH) had reached even distant territories, so that even people from remote locations rushed to visit him and before he was sent as a prophet, they heralded this position to him. Prophet Mohammad (PBUH) is a clear example of a person who has reached from unawareness to self-awareness and absolute faith lies with him without seeing God. In fact, he saw God through the manifestation of God in nature and this world, because the world and nature, as well as man himself, are a mirror of the wonder and necessity of superior power.

Prophet Mohammad (PBUH) recounted what he received by his heart and in his mindful principles (inspiration and revelation) to the people and scribes to be recorded and written for others and future generations. From the point of view of those who do not believe in the revelation or command of God to guide and instruct people and to send a prophet, and think that the issue of the prophecy is only the institutionalization of fantasies and becoming their belief, the question may arise why doesn't God prevent it? One answer could be this: for the same reason that it has not prevented many of the strange and horrific oppressions and catastrophes that have befallen human beings throughout human life. Because after the creation of order and the heavens, the earth and the other planets, moving in a certain direction according to the pre-determined laws and principles, He no longer see the need for further interference and occupation in the affairs. He allow every possible action to happen and every event to occur until the Day of Judgment; Good or bad; He must be comfortable with the fact that everything will be recorded. It is as if nature itself has taken over, even if man separates the head of another virtuous man from the body, God does not intervene. Why does God not interfere with the affairs of the world and allow the next events to inevitably take place after the rules and regulations of nature, and everything possible to happen in the direction of nature. I do not know the answer to this question either. Therefore, there is no reason for God to stop good deeds, such as the prophets who recited his unspoken words and promoted a better way of life in the direction of the straight path, so God will be pleased with these events. Undoubtedly, God does not like people to worship him out of fear or out of greed for paradise, maybe that is the reason why He is hidden from view and could not understood and could not fall into delusion.

On the other hand, it is possible that God made an exception for the sending of prophets and really revealed the true manifestation of himself or his angels to the prophets.

If human beings are guided only by pure conscience, compassion, love for fellow human beings and other creatures, beauty and semantics in completely free conditions and without coercion and external factors, to a straight path and self-awareness in such a way that dust and smoke prevent seeing the truth, remove, Then the pleasure of God is obtained. We may even be led to the straight path and self-awareness and blurring of vision without reading the scriptures and religious teachings because suffering is a doctor, it is enough to do what we know is good and not to do what we know is bad. Man has an esoteric messenger who guides him.

Of course, the universe is so big and the planets are so small that God may not even be aware of the existence of smaller particles called the living organisms. There may be other worlds that, if viewed from above (from the point of view of the Creator of the worlds), can only be seen in multiple worlds and not within worlds, let alone the Milky Way galaxy, which is nothing more than a particle in our universe and in relation to the universe is extremely tiny. He may guess that creatures can be created through materials in nature, but He does not have the statistics, or He may be searching for creatures and finding some of them. If He does not find it, He may despair and destroy the existing worlds and create other worlds.

As a future research, you can do research in this regard which religion and the prophet has established the basic principles and laws that are mentioned in the last divine religion from the Muslims' perspective, namely Islam, for the first time in the evolution of religions, the oneness of God and also the weakness of the god of evil over the god of goodness and the transformation of the god of evil into a creature called Satan who is the son of a good god and also the promise of a savior and the story of the rise and fall of Adam and Eve, etc. The answer to this question reveals which religion or prophet first coordinated the current theology and established the final framework for religions and the ultimate theology.

The reason for divine tests and the multiplicity of human beings and the formulation of a hypothesis

If I had died at the age of 26, I might have been taken to a lower place in that world because I had done less good deeds, but now that I have reached the age of 38, I may have reached greater intellectual maturity, perhaps after my death and go to a better place. This is how human aging will affect human beings to go to heaven or hell. Is a person who dies as an innocent child and will go to heaven, or should a person who grew up in different circumstances like a criminal go to hell? Maybe if we were in his place, we would act like him, but because we are not, we will go to heaven for our actions due to different circumstances and situations; is this justice?!!! It seems that this is far from fair and just, the person who has stolen something may have really been forced to do so, or for some reason, the fear of stealing has been taken away from him, or the taste of stealing the property of others has pleased him/her. Possibly, if we were in his place and we put our feet in his shoes and walked by them, we would behave like him and be like him, so it is not fair for such a person to go to hell and we go to heaven. The best model can be on average the behavior of all human beings and then turn to human society (both dead and alive and human beings who were not and will not be created at all). The greater the number of samples and tests, the higher the accuracy of the sampling, and finally the approximate conclusion can be drawn about a human being or creature and the true nature of his existence. In other words, at the end of this story, only one human being may remain as the representative of all human beings created on the planet, in which case the conclusion and comment on the true nature of human beings will be relative and will depend on the number of samples and the type and amount of tests. Therefore, a definite and absolute conclusion is not possible.

The heavenly books do not speak of the immortal soul and the resurrection of other animals, and the immortal soul is intended only for humans, because other animals are eaten by humans and are a means of human survival in this world. A major difference between humans and other animals is that the range of decline as well as the intellectual and moral development of modern man is much wider than that of other animals.

Adam and Eve

According to the heavenly scriptures, it seems that from the beginning, many humans were not supposed to be created, and only Adam and Eve were enough, but after committing a mistake against God's command, they were expelled from heaven. Thus it is understood that birth and reproduction began from that time. So, from that time on, many people were supposed to open their eyes to the world. Be born and then die, because that is how civilizations came into being and human beings can be tested in different situations, for example by having a neighbor, friend, acquaintance, employer or subordinate worker who creates relationships. There are different actions, challenges and actions. It is in interactions with other human beings that human beings can be tested. At the same time, it is far from fair and just that Adam and Eve were tested billions of times, so it was necessary for many human beings to be born with a seemingly empty memory and to be tested and tested and then killed and again. Be born with a seemingly empty memory; In such a way that they do not bear the burden of grief for many years. But when all human beings are gathered on the Day of Judgment, the sum of their behavior and actions may be averaged. In other words, to be studied and analyzed in a scientific and research way. In scientific, statistical methods, the number of samples should be large enough to cover the statistical community.

All the dead may eventually become one or two (Adam and Eve), the very first humans at the beginning of human creation.

Since the reason for the creation of all of us human beings (except Adam and Eve) was due to the mistake of Adam and Eve, who acted contrary to God's commands, from the beginning, it was intended that only Adam and Eve were created and we were to prove their legitimacy and further experiments have opened our eyes to this world, so in the end we may all be reunited in the form of one or two. By combining all the actions and deeds of human beings so that in total and by averaging and calculating and scientific-statistical conclusions, a more logical and fair judgment can be made about a person (one or two people). Each of us, in turn, has a role to play in this divine test, depending on the circumstances as well as the abilities, talents, chances, and games of the times that we will encounter. A set of rules and principles in this world through the soul or body, mind, world, earth, elements, emotions (such as: love, jealousy, sadness, grief, regret, hope, greed, passion, desire, etc.) to we are dictated to be like algebra. Also, the authority and power to decide in different situations through reason shape our behaviors and actions. In most cases, these actions are largely predictable, meaning that a person with certain characteristics, personality, and civilization is expected to do so.

In other words, the future behaviors and actions of human beings are largely predictable by knowing the people and society in which they live, and God knows human beings and human society, and also knows that if He has provided the present conditions for a person, this is the reason, It's that person's behavior and actions, so it is easier for God to judge him than us. We are may not be aware of his past situations and circumstances.

According to Darwin's theory, man was not created all at once and as it is taken from the heavenly books, but gradually and more complex than single-celled and multi-celled, and then by natural selection compatible with the environment and the removal of incomplete or incompatible with the nature and evolved from animals. Based on archaeological and ecological evidence and the study of animals in different geographical environments, as well as genetic studies, many biologists agree with Darwin's theory. In such cases, doubts about the authenticity of the scriptures or doubts about Darwin's theory would be more pleasing and logical for religious people than doubts about superior power.

Do you forgive God?

It can be imagined that, as soon as we exist, this is a tragedy in itself (as opposed to the view that existence is the greatest blessing), at least in this material world it seems. For a long time I thought that God was unforgivable, but now I think that God is forgiving because He has put something called death on his agenda and may compensate in the next world. Of course, man has the right to doubt salvation and happiness in the next world, because the mechanism of this world is such that it does not show us a good picture of God's treatment of human beings because of its strictness. So man has the right to be pessimistic about happiness in the next world as well, because we have once experienced existence in this material world on earth, and in this way we have gained a slight acquaintance with God. The consequences of living in this world (on Earth) can be a sense of pessimism about the next world.

But in any case, both God and parents are forgivable, but I do not know that God forgives parents. Because parents, in spite of living in this world and experiencing the conditions and mechanisms of this world, have nevertheless tried to have children and have not been taught a lesson. By having children, we may cause our grandchildren to suffer. Of course, this action may be forgivable, especially since it is a wisdom to become parents and also to improve and orient the way of life and human perfection, as well as to practice loving and forgiving one's interests for another one, it seems to have this style of life- is the ultimate purpose of God.

Pain sufferer is a doctor

It is a saying that "pain sufferer is a doctor". Suffering makes us uncomfortable and we like to avoid it, it is interesting that we extend it to our own kind and other animals and feel sympathy with them as if they are also an integral part and in direct contact with us. In other words, we have a connection with other animals and humans. In the words of the great Iranian poet Saadi:

Human beings are members of a whole,

In creation of one essence and soul.

If one member is afflicted with pain,

Other members uneasy will remain.

We want others to understand and approve of us, to think with us, and even to share in our joys and sorrows. If someone is struggling, our hearts will burn for him and we would like to help him, all this is in the shadow of our grace and cream of suffering and pain. The mechanism of this world is such that suffering and sorrow are the prerequisites and necessities of human perfection from the perspective of the Lord of the universe. Hunger and fasting are to remember the hungry (and of course to enjoy eating after the hardships of hunger), sickness and calamity are to be in a situation where if someone else gets it, we can understand it (of course, because of the value of health, as well as remembering how weak and vulnerable we are) and experience it in advance. This feeling of grief and compassion for others may develop so much that a free person is willing to go beyond his own interests and help others. In other words, to sacrifice for the benefit of another or to prefer collective interests to individual interests. Therefore, a suffering human being can achieve a high standard of cure.

Obviously, the purpose of creation is not to achieve a dose of medicine through enduring pain and suffering, but it is just one of the solutions and paths, the other path is to taste the pleasures and feelings of happiness that are effective in becoming a doctor. For example, if you enjoy delicious food, you would like others to enjoy this gift and have a common feeling with you and align in common feelings so that you can have a common understanding of each other and be led to collective wisdom. So the feeling of joy and happiness make you think that life is worth continuing and surviving, and you wish happiness and joy to others, which shows love and humanity, so what strengthens the spirit of humanity and love in you is the same as living and being happy and enjoying the pleasure of the world by yourself that makes you love yourself, making others feel happy.

Humans inadvertently suffer and bear; in fact, there may be no reason to grieve.

Apart from the physical pain that inevitably puts pressure on the brain nerves and can only be controlled through the use of painkillers or anesthesia, the rest of the pain and suffering we suffer is mental and can be controlled by ourselves, of course, psychedelic pills. They help a lot, but they can be prevented through the power of the mind. It is unfortunate that human beings grieve or suffer, emotional suffering is due to our own imaginations and thoughts. We suffer because of things like insatiability, extravagance, greediness, lust, malice, jealousy, selfishness, regret, and so on. In fact, we are the ones who oppress ourselves, among other factors, we can mention the suffering and hardship of friends and relatives, which causes us to be reminded that like stress, which is harmful but also has benefits, it helps each of us also has a law book of our own belief system and an inner judge through which we reprimand and punish ourselves over and over for an illegal act or mistake, while a judge for a Mistakes punish the offender only once, but the inner judge does this to us over and over again, and in this way we absorb negative energies. The English speakers have a saying: "take it easy", because it makes you live happily and cheerfully.

The main culprit is our own suffering and unhappy life, we are the human beings who border the planet with countries and make ourselves more limited and confined and we cannot easily enter other countries. Each country pursues its own interests and even oppresses other countries, fights with each other and kills its own kind (of course, they have many benefits for each other through imports, exports and exchange of knowledge) and also Within societies within a country, it is we humans who can make the planet a better place to live, not just for a few, but for the majority or the whole of human society and other beings.

We limit ourselves and do not use our existing abilities and facilities properly and adequately, so that we waste our opportunities. Civilizations also increase our restrictions on living freely by enacting laws to govern affairs.

Just as stress has destructive effects on the body and soul, but it causes a person to react in a timely manner, for example, to do more study for the test, or to be cautious in matters, and also to think about the consequences. So, being regretful of the past, worrying about the future, suffering spontaneously, and all our sorrows and grieves, in addition to the negative effects and aspects they have, can have wisdom and cause us to learn a lesson as well as promote us to achieve an ultimate goal.

If one realizes that the world is not worth grieving and that we are just a small traveler of time, as well as the belief that we can live happier and that we are the cause of our sorrow and suffering, which is due to our mental imaginations and inspirations, he will never again go for sorrow and grief, but he will try to go towards joys and absorb positive energy. Grief comes to you anyway, so you try to go to joys.

Man oppresses himself, by entering into a mortal and transient world that is not blinking in the eye. Learn to live like children in the present and in the moment, not to regret the past and not to worry about the future, and not to forget that we are mortal and will die.

Other restrictions that lead to the deprivation of liberty imposed on human societies are the laws, covenants, and customs of a society that force its members to live within a certain framework and to live their lives, the norms that Existing societies make a person subject to a collective, civilized and cultured. In this way he discovers himself in the form of that society and perhaps distances himself from the real self he should have been. How original and consistent is civilization and culture? How good or bad? Why are humans limited and how much is it good or bad for them? (Of course, religious principles and rules also play an important role in guiding culture and civilization). Doesn't that make humans live mechanically and automatically? Running a living full of stress and anxiety away from nature and the sky, is it sufficient to just imagine that we are free to socialize as long as we do not harm others? While this sentence is worth considering that "whatever you do not like for yourself, do not like for others, and whatever you like for yourself, like for others". We are also a part of nature itself and belong to it in a way that relaxes us and removes negative energy and absorbs positive energy. The farther we go from nature and the existential nature of man himself, the less positive energy there will be and the more negative energy there will be, and vice versa.

Sometimes we have to play like children, experience excitement and pleasure, live in the present to realize that life means these short moments of joy that pass. Time is fluid and flowing so that you can swim and surf. It is enough to lighten ourselves and float on it, a lot of paddling will waste our energy and fatigue. Enjoy every moment of your life. The greatest revenge you can take on this world is to live happily.

In any case, one should try not to think about things with negative energy and do not go for it, but take a step towards positivity and absorb only positive energy. Get enough sleep, travel, sometimes eat ice cream or even chips, reconcile with nature, do all the other positive energy activities you deem appropriate, such as: watching movies and cartoons, listening to music, playing games, love humans. hobbies such as cooking, going to the fridge and licking your mouth, visiting relatives and friends, watching the sky, trees, mountains, sea and other wonders of nature, etc ... Also know that everything has a period that If it passes, it may lose its freshness and pleasure, such as watching cartoons as a child that was a world to us, or traveling in old age may be difficult and tedious.

Good Gene

It is possible that in the future, good genes taken from smart and well-built people will be used abundantly for fertility and reproduction, because this world could be a better place to live, which requires the growth of science and technology. As well as the growth of civilization and culture and things like that. Humans have reached some of these results, but it is not long before humans move away from selfishness and focus more on future generations. I think that one day human beings will finally come to the conclusion that using good genes to continue the human race is a logical and beneficial thing, and this wisdom and expediency will one day overcome the selfishness of human beings. This has happened more widely for some animals, such as cows, which use sperm with good genes to fertilize cows to lead to more milk and meat. Plant breeding, which is done through genetic manipulation, is also being done in abundance. In addition to using good genes, future generations may also be genetically engineered, which is not yet operational due to ethical issues and fear of consequences. But sperm with good genes are sometimes used. It is also possible that after passing through the above stage, humans will come to the conclusion that reproduction and continuation of generation is oppression against human beings, thus preventing the continuation of generation or the destruction of living beings. Although unlikely, it is not impossible.

Is there heaven and hell?

Wherever time pleases, there is paradise. There is a lot of talk in the heavenly books about heaven and hell, but since no one has returned from that world, how happy heaven is and how horrible hell is, is just a fantasy from the mind. It passes and only God knows how true these ideas and fantasies are. Since man has lived in this world and has the experience of living in this world, he analyzes and compares the next world with this world, which of course seems to be wrong, but what God does with human beings in this world And with this background and history that has already afflicted human beings in hardships and difficulties, of course, along with the happy and sweet moments, it can be an indication that God has this ability and talent that if He wants, He may inflict torment And provide conditions for happiness and joy. In terms of lasting happiness and abundant possibilities, one must see what the capacity and aspect of human beings is. Do humans expect to be immersed in lasting happiness? It is not unlikely. But as for hell, which I think is just a mental image, it is unlikely for God to disturb His creatures more than they can bear and for a long time, which He created in the best way, in such a way that the prince of creatures was created and breathed into it by the Spirit of God. Of course, in this world he suffers, however, it is transient and mortal, and following the hardships, there have also been blissful moments. If He hurts a person who has the spirit of God, He is actually hurting himself. If He understands human beings, then He will also be aware of their suffering and sorrow and himself will be hurt. If it is otherwise, that is, do not be offended, and then we also have the right to object to God and tell him, you who were not in our place, why have you not yet become a living being or a human being and experience a lowly life on earth? Did not you? So why are you so hard on your creatures? Is it the creature that you have created, is it fair to test what you have created by force and compulsion, in any way you want? While you were not in their place and in the Throne (heaven) your heart is a pill without any sorrow. Should not a person be asked before birth if he would like to enter this world?

While we have not even been asked and we have entered this world by force and then we will die. Is it fair to enter the world by force and enter the game of the times and die? In this world, let us suffer, try and be tested, but do not even ask us if you are willing to enter the game of life? And finally, we have to be reprimanded and held accountable for our actions. Would not God Himself have done the same behaviors and actions according to the nature of creation and the attraction and lure of the world and being material? We are, in fact, a mirror of God Himself, we are God Himself, because His Spirit has been breathed into us, so if any movement arises from us, it is God Himself who, through intermediaries and in material circumstances, emerges from Him. It is God who has manifested himself in another form. We are God, but only a manifestation or particle of it, and not a perfect God, but created from anime, and without God we will disappear and our existence will have no meaning. If so, then God is still alive and not dead because we are and feel or exist. So as long as we feel there is God. But if God has changed his whole being in the form of another form and has used all his existence to create the world and living beings, then this world will continue to follow the path and its representative that living beings are to understand the universe. All may be merely a transfiguration of the Lord's sacred nature, which in the future will return to its original nature and return to a state in which the stars and this world did not exist.

I wish God could transform himself into a human being and live on this planet for a few days like us. With the same hardships and difficulties, as well as the limited mind and with the same ignorance and low intelligence, it may be necessary for him to be a better judge in the Hereafter. Not, for example, to compare us with him or the angels or the prophets and determine what we deserve. Has this world been pleasing to us? Have we been entitled to it? In any case, if we have chosen to be ourselves and live in this world and come to our own free will, then God will have the right to test us. That is, our suffering is the atonement of being human, and this world is like a school that is a prerequisite for higher levels of science and education. But if we are created by force and we are forced to go through the stages of progress and prosperity by force, this is an injustice to human rights, especially if we are not proud and successful in the divine test, so that we will be subject to hell and punishment. This is not in line with any argument and fairness, and it is pure oppression. There is something fishy. To solve this problem, three hypotheses can be considered. *One*, man himself has accepted to be created, and by generation, he affirms this, because instead of learning a lesson, he keeps on generation, and affirms his desire for his own creation (of course, there are examples of violations, such as people who do not want to have children). *Second*, there is no hell in the Hereafter, and God has raised this issue only to frighten human beings. The hell of this world is just our forged thoughts and fantasies that have made the world hell for us. It is a delusion because we have been deceived by time, while perhaps time only exists from our point of view and is made for us, and in the blink of an eye it will pass and we will die. Perhaps life in this world is much shorter than we think, and it has actually extends to us. *Three,* Something like the theory of reincarnation in the end of this story the behavior and deeds of humans will be averaged and the balance is referred to Adam and Eve i.e. the two first humans.

As a research topic think about whether it is better to pray "God have mercy on him" or to say "God make his soul happy".

How much do we know about God? How far is it from imagining and knowing God to the truth?

No one has seen God directly, and it is impossible for a weak being like man to be able to see God with these physical characteristics. But the belief in the existence of a superior and creative power of the universe is strengthened by observing the world and nature. The whole universe is in fact a miracle that reflects the existence of a superior power to drive it. Because we know God through nature and the universe, so our knowledge of God is incomplete and in fact we are unaware of His other powers as well as His form and image, but we have some knowledge of His holy nature, we know He has attributes such as wise, judicious, kind, gracious, patient, etc. Of course, it is also thought that God is a superior power that has been unkind and harsh to man in this world. The above traits are understandable because they are common to human traits. But if God has attributes that are not in common with the attributes of human beings, we will not be able to understand and be unaware of it. It is possible that God has more attributes than human beings that cannot be described and understood, so we will be completely unaware of the hidden halves of God and may remain in this ignorance forever. Everything we have discovered or seen in this world belongs only to this universe, while God may have already created other worlds and is doing more than this universe and for the same reason as if it were news of he's not. If a creature creates a better being than man, it may no longer be a reason to motivate man in the next world. After all, our knowledge of God is shaped by the scriptures, as well as our need for a higher power as well as the wonders of the world. Since each person's perception of God's attributes differs, no one knows God as he really is, as if there are as many people as there are people on earth, but God is all one and the same power. It is our perception that is incomplete and different.

In the famous saying, "If you come to yourself, you will reach a god." That is, man must first know himself and then know God. From infancy, self-knowledge is acquired over time, and the personality of human beings at older ages is stabilized by experiencing the cold and the warmth of the times.

The story of our lives

Life in this world is like a story in which each of us plays a role in this story. With every decision we make, the direction of this story changes, and perhaps it moves toward what has already been predetermined, that is, predicted or even predetermined. It is because of the need for the story to happen that others are pushing you to the direction of righteousness, such as getting married, studying, having fun, enjoy yourself, or anything else they are used to or dreaming of, and or engage with it in their bell. That is, everyone has somehow preserved the story of life. But you do not have to follow the life story that others prescribe. You can choose your own way, and that is how the life story changes and a new story emerges while it is still a story. It remains to be seen whether this story is better and more interesting than the previous one. In any case, using the experience of others should not be forgotten.

For those who have no belief in the Hereafter

One has to ask such people, do you have any belief in this world and do you exist at all and touch the world around you? If their answer is yes, then it must be said that such a world came into being or pre-existed and such beings were created, and it was very difficult to believe, but it is possible and it exists and it seems quite real. While it is hard to believe that such a world exists with these characteristics, it seems like a dream or a miracle. Maybe it's a dream. Nor should anything be possible, while it seems perfectly obvious and conceivable and hard to deny.

Last Word

In the end, we are reminded again and again to ring a bell every day that *we are a small time traveler* so that we may broaden our horizons, and this makes us look at things from above and look at the world delightfully, using this method will cause dramatic changes in human mindsets in relation to the events and the world around them. Another piece of advice is to read books, to read good books, to read books well, and don't forget to think when you are alone.

Country Flowers

A Pocket Guide to

Common British Wildflowers.

Sally Featherstone

Country Flowers

ISBN 9781838003555

words and pictures by
Sally Featherstone

First published by Opitus Books, United Kingdom, 2021.

Introduction

Country Flowers was inspired by the book '**Flora,** *ten years among the flowers of an endangered landscape',* which describes the unique range of flowers growing in seven small fields on the hills above the Calder Valley in West Yorkshire. Readers of Flora, while enjoying the quality of the full sized, lavishly illustrated volume, with its 400 colour photos and detailed context, said they would find a pocket-sized version of the individual flower pages useful to take with them on walks through the Pennine countryside and the hay meadows of West Yorkshire.

Country Flowers has been compiled to contain all the flowers from Flora, expanded to include a wider range of common British wildflowers. Each page carries essential information to help you to identify individual flowers from their key features, including colour photographs, the Latin name, some of the country names, which are often more amusing and descriptive than the official ones, the size and colour of the flower, historical and herbal details, and fascinating facts about each one.

Some pages have a warning on toxicity - such as dangerous irritant sap, or other features that make it wise to avoid picking or eating them. These warnings are in red.

Most plants will cope with gentle handling, but picking wildflowers should usually be avoided. They are a valuable resource for birds and insects, and they will never look as beautiful when you get them home as they do in their natural habitat. Even carefully arranged in water, they do not last, as they are not used to indoor life.

However, children have now become so conscious of protecting the environment that they are anxious about picking _any_ flower, and the result is that many children can't recognise or name common wildflowers and insects so familiar to their parents and grandparents. Wildflower charities, such as Plantlife and The Woodland Trust, now recommend that we should encourage our youngest children to gather the most plentiful of these wildflowers, such as Buttercups, Dandelions and Daisies, just as we did when we were children. A list of these 'child friendly' flowers is in the back of this Guide. Other flowers in this collection, including Bluebells and Orchids are endangered or have protected status, and should not be picked. Please help your children to learn their names and help to protect them.

Many of the flowers in this collection grow among the grasses or at the margins of meadows and footpaths in West and South Yorkshire, in the Calder Valley and the Peak District where I now live. In these places wild flowers still bloom in profusion, and if you are lucky enough to find one of these secret meadows, particularly when the flowers are at their best, please ask the owner's permission before entering them. They are endangered habitats, and could be permanently damaged by trampling or picking the flowers, or even walking among them. We must preserve the places where wildflowers grow, so our children and grandchildren can enjoy them too.

Living through a pandemic has made us all appreciate the countryside so much more, and we know that taking time to stop and look in detail at nature can improve both our mental and physical health.